To Lausie

With thanks for the kindness you've
shown my son & heir, and in the
hope you don't take the Moses Maclar
quote too seriously.

SO-BYN-086

Other anthologies of quotations by Gordon S. Jackson

Never Scratch a Tiger With a Short Stick – And Other Quotations for Leaders

Outside Insights – Quotes for Contemporary South Africa

Quotes for the Journey, Wisdom for the Way

The Weather is Here, Wish You Were Beautiful – Quotations for the Thoughtful Traveler

Watchdogs, Blogs and Wild Hogs – A Collection of Quotations on Media

Sleep Faster, We Need the Pillows

Sleep Faster, We Need the Pillows

500 Logical Lapses, Paradoxes and Other Mental Delights

[signature]

Compiled by Gordon S. Jackson

Copyright © 2012 Gordon S. Jackson
All rights reserved.

Except as permitted by applicable copyright laws, no
part of this book may be reproduced, duplicated, sold or
distributed in any form or by any means, either
mechanical, by photocopy, electronic, or by computer, or
stored in a database or retrieval system, without the
express permission of the compiler, except for brief
quotations by reviewers.

Printed in the USA by Create Space
2012

Library of Congress Control Number: 2012950127

ISBN: 1479300403
ISBN-13:978-1479300402

Cover design by Sarah E. Jackson

Dedication

To Janeso and Jamie, for their
extraordinary generosity

Acknowledgements

This collection of paradoxes, ambiguities and other "logical lapses" is indebted to the help of several individuals. My colleague at Whitworth University, philosophy professor Nathan King put me in touch with some of his discipline's literature on paradoxes. He also offered feedback on this project. So did other friends and colleagues, including Sarah Bain, Carl Green, Jeff Haschick, Mike Ingram, Philemon Nkabinde, Kyle Storm, and Joy York.

Gail Fielding, in Whitworth University's library, once again procured useful resources on inter-library loan. Another colleague, Laura Reber, helped me to work the kinks out of the manuscript and tried to calm me as I did battle with MS Word and its perverse eccentricities.

My wife, Sue, made various comments that helped me to refine the manuscript – as did my son, Matthew, and daughter, Sarah, who also designed the book's cover. My friend, Kathy Watts, provided indispensible help in steering me through the on-line preparation of the e-copy of this book.

Then, Denise Han, a Whitworth student, merits my thanks for her indispensible role in helping me to sort, order and check the quotations that comprise this volume.

But the greatest debt of course goes to those writers and speakers who made this volume possible. Whether through their brilliant wit or inadvertent verbal blunders, the logical lapses compiled here would not exist but for them. (I've said more about them in the Introduction.)

Great care has been taken in the selection of the quotations that follow to honor the fair use doctrine in copyright law. If any inadvertent omissions have occurred in this regard, these will be addressed in possible future editions of this book.

Introduction

"After all, what was a paradox but a statement of the obvious so as to make it sound untrue."
– R. A. Knox

"Paradoxes are fun," says philosopher R. M. Sainsbury. "In most cases, they are easy to state and immediately provoke one into trying to 'solve' them." And that's the dual objective of this anthology: Each quotation here is intended to provide you with some fun and to challenge your thinking, offering an opportunity for playfulness and delight as you read a statement that seems to make sense while obviously sounding wrong at the same time.

Each quote has been selected because it holds some inherent tension that leads to some kind of double-take, making you say, "Huh?" or its equivalent. The quotes include well known self-referential paradoxes, like the statement, "This sentence is false," or the ancient paradoxical statement by Epimenedes of Crete, "All Cretans are liars." Most, though, are likely to be unfamiliar. But whether you recognize them or not, all the quotes have been selected for their potential to stimulate your thinking in some way, with each offering its own "mini-mental workout" as it invites you to understand or explain or perhaps simply delight in the thinking behind it.

More modern ones include several by Groucho Marx, including his resignation from a club because, he said, "I don't care to belong to any social organization that will accept me as a member." You will also probably be familiar with his other contributions, and those by those two 20th century icons of illogicality, Yogi Berra and Samuel Goldwyn. Of course, how many of the quotes attributed to Goldwyn are authentic is another matter. His less-than-fluent English undoubtedly led to many mangled misstatements, but it's also widely accepted that Metro-Goldwyn-Mayer's public relations staff coined examples for which their boss got credit. They're included here because the mangling of language, whether intended or not, constitute a genre of their own. The same applies to baseball legend Yogi Berra.

In general, though, logical mistakes by well known figures have been kept to a minimum. This volume could easily have been filled with the misstatements of former President George W. Bush and, before him, by former Vice President Dan Quayle. In recognition of their contribution to the amusement of English-speakers everywhere, a token contribution from each of these has been included.

The emphasis in the collection, though, is on quotations that are *intended* to be thought provoking in some way. Hence the Yiddish proverb: "If the rich could hire other people to die for them, the poor could make a wonderful living." Or the delicious ambiguity of British Prime Minister Benjamin Disraeli's comment in parliament: "Mr. Speaker, I withdraw my statement that half the cabinet are asses – half the cabinet are not asses."

This anthology is thus populated mostly with epigrams, aphorisms, or deliberately paradoxical or ambiguous statements. Also included are the occasional anecdote, like Quentin Crisp's recollection: "When I told the people of Northern Ireland I was an atheist, a woman in the audience stood up and said, 'Yes, but is it the God of the Catholics or the God of the Protestants in whom you don't believe?'" Some entries, like the few limericks that have fun parodying that strict five-line format, won't meet a purist's definition of a "logical lapse." Just enjoy them anyway, or else move on.

I have mostly resisted including the "bumper sticker" one-liners that kept circulating in cyberspace shortly after we discovered how to forward e-mails. Here too, though, I made exceptions. This line merits inclusion: "I went to buy some camouflage trousers but I couldn't find any." By contrast, I decided that phrases like "monosyllabic isn't" – attractive though it is at first glance – was too superficial or predictable for inclusion. Similarly, I decided that most oxymorons ("pretty ugly" or "peacekeeping force") didn't require the mini-mental workout that I wanted to characterize each quotation.

Where do the quotes come from? The quotes are almost entirely from print sources, with only a few from some of the more authoritative Internet sites. Besides the "logical lapses" quotes I have collected over the years, I have scoured numerous books on logic, paradoxes and word puzzles, as well as scores of other anthologies of quotations. I am especially indebted to writers whose books on paradoxes and logical puzzles initially spurred my motivation to collect quotations on this topic. In particular, I have benefited from Martin Gardner's *Aha! Gotcha: Paradoxes to*

Puzzle and Delight; Robert Martin's *There are Two Errors in The The Title of This Book*; R. M. Sainsbury's *Paradoxes*; Raymond Smullyan's two volumes, *What is the Name of this Book?* and *This Book Needs no Title*; and Roy Sorenson's *Brief History of the Paradox*.

These authors, of course, are smart enough that they can *explain* the kinds of logical problems that lie behind these quotes. Just as a skilled music reviewer can tell us why a piece of music was performed well (or not), so too do these writers help us understand why the kind of quotes contained here are logical conundrums.

This compilation is therefore indebted to their insights and observations and those of hundreds of other writers and thinkers over the ages. Not surprisingly, comedians and comedy writers have a special gift for playing with ideas that often lead to delightful illogicalities, like Bob Monkhouse's statement that, "They laughed when I said I was going to be a comedian. They're not laughing now." Other comedians featured prominently here include Woody Allen, Groucho Marx, Spike Milligan (the late British comic genius little known in the United States), and Steven Wright.

While this anthology is not a scholarly work, I have put a high premium on accuracy. Where a quote is attributed to more than one individual, I have relied on the source that appears most authoritative. Then there is the issue of inclusive language. Some quotes use "man," "mankind" and so on when referring to people in general. These quotes reflect earlier usage which characterizes contemporary English less and less. In keeping with the volume's commitment to presenting the quotes as accurately as possible, I have included these entries with their original wording. Most of the sources are given without any further details, but where I thought it would be helpful to understand the context I have briefly described the source or otherwise provided some background details.

Back to Sainsbury. He notes that while paradoxes can indeed be entertaining, for philosophers they are a serious business. He tells how the "Liar Paradox" (see the section on Logic, Truth and Lies) "tormented many ancient logicians..." – even causing the premature death of Philetus of Cos. It's hard to imagine what he would have made of this collection. My hope is that, far from following Philetus's example, you will derive only enjoyment from the quotations that follow.

The Topics

Advice

Eschew obfuscation.
— Norman Augustine

Hear what they are not saying.
— Steve de Masco

The greatest mistake you can make in life is to be continually fearing you will make one.
— Elbert Hubbard

There are two rules for success in life:
1. Don't tell people everything you know.
2.
— Roger H. Lincoln

The people sensible enough to give good advice are usually sensible enough to give none.
— Eden Phillpotts

Ages and Aging

Youth would be an ideal state if it came later in life.
— Lord Asquith

I'm not young enough to know everything.
— James Barrie

If you live to the age of a hundred, you have it made because very few people die past the age of a hundred.
— George Burns

A witness cannot give evidence of his age unless he can remember being born.
— Judge William Collis Blagdon

The really frightening thing about middle age is the knowledge that you'll grow out of it.
— Doris Day

By the time you are in mid-career your "experience" will have been gained in a world that no longer exists.
— Irwin Miller

I think age is a very high price to pay for maturity.
— Tom Stoppard

It takes about ten years to get used to how old you are.
— Unknown

Ambiguous Recommendations
(Source unknown)

He is definitely a young man to watch.

I am pleased to say this candidate is a former colleague of mine.

I most enthusiastically recommend this man with no qualifications whatsoever.

No salary will be too much for her.

There's nothing you can teach a man like him.

You will be very fortunate to get him to work for you.

America and Americans

America is so vast that almost everything said about it is likely to be true, and the opposite is probably equally true.
— James T. Farrell

Part of the American dream is to live long and die young.
— Edgar Z. Friedenberg

The United States has to move very fast to even stand still.
— John Kennedy

The greatest American superstition is belief in facts.
— Hermann Keyserling

Never criticize Americans. They have the best taste money can buy.
— Miles Kington

In America everybody is but some are more than others. I was more than others.
— Gertrude Stein, on her celebrity status in the United States

See also **G. K. Chesterton** *and* **Oscar Wilde**

Appearances

Admiring Friend: "My, that's a beautiful baby you have there!"
Mother: "Oh, that's nothing – you should see his photograph."
— cited by Daniel Boorstin

The best thing is to look natural, but it takes makeup to look natural.
— Calvin Klein

Could you tell if, one day, everything in the universe suddenly doubled in size?
— Robert M. Martin

You were conspicuous by your absence.
— Lord John Russell

This is either a forgery or a damn clever original!
— Frank Sullivan

Well, it looks like a Rorschach inkblot to me.
— Unknown

It's not an optical illusion, it just looks like one.
— Phil White

The Arts

I liked your opera. I think I will set it to music.
— Ludwig van Beethoven, to a fellow composer

In the theatre, people want to be surprised – but by things they expect.
— Tristan Bernard

This film is apparently meaningless, but if it has any meaning it is doubtless objectionable.
— British Board of Film Censors, banning Jean Cocteau's film *The Seashells and the Clergyman*, 1956

Poetry lies its way to the truth.
— John Ciardi

People are wrong when they say the opera isn't what it used to be. It is what it used to be. That's what's wrong with it.
— Noël Coward

It's taken me all my life to learn what not to play.
— Dizzy Gillespie

The best screen actor is one who can do nothing supremely well.
— Alfred Hitchcock

Hook and Ladder is the sort of play that gives failures a bad name.
— Walter Kerr

Why have you come into my show, austere Cato? Pray, did you walk in merely for the purpose of walking out?
— Martial

Not reading poetry amounts to a national pastime here.
— Phyllis McGinley

Art is a lie that makes us realize the truth.
— Pablo Picasso

Every act of creation is first an act of destruction.
— Pablo Picasso

When I was a kid I drew like Michelangelo. It took me years to learn to draw like a kid.
— Pablo Picasso

The sonatas of Mozart are unique; they are too easy for children, and too difficult for artists.
— Arthur Schnabel

This is a show which you must not fail to miss.
— Unknown reviewer

Writing about music is like dancing about architecture.
— Unknown

Critics search for ages for the wrong word, which, to give them credit, they eventually find.
— Peter Ustinov

I started at the top and worked my way down.
— Orson Welles

Yogi Berra

I never said half the things I really said.

If the people don't want to come out to the park, nobody's gonna stop them.

If you come to a fork in the road, take it.

If you've ever suffered from insomnia you'll know what a nightmare it is.

It's déjà vu all over again.

Nobody goes there anymore; it's too crowded.

You can observe a lot by watching.

You've got to be very careful if you don't know where you're going, because you might not get there.

Books and Reading

I haven't read everything I wrote.
— Karl Barth, prolific theologian's
possibly apocryphal response to a
student who claimed he'd read
everything Barth had written

A best seller . . . is a book known
primarily (sometimes exclusively) for its
well-knownness.
— Daniel Boorstin

Thank you for sending me a copy of your
book. I shall waste no time reading it.
— Moses Hadas

Some people read because they are too
lazy to think.
— Lichtenberg

*There are Two Errors in the the Title of
this Book*
— Book by Robert M. Martin

I never read a book before reviewing it;
it prejudices a man so.
— Sydney Smith

What is the Name of This Book?
This Book Needs No Title
— Two books by Raymond Smullyan

Change

Everything is in a state of flux,
including the status quo.
— Robert Byrne

Happy is the one who understands the
necessity of changing to remain always
oneself.
— Dom Hélder Câmara

There is nothing permanent except
change.
— Heraclitus

Progress might have been all right once but it has gone on too long.
— Ogden Nash

The curious paradox is that when I accept myself just as I am, then I can change.
— Carl Rogers

Sixty years of progress without change.
— Saudi Arabian government slogan to promote the Kingdom's 60th anniversary

G. K. Chesterton

Bigotry may be roughly defined as the anger of men who have no opinions.

If a thing is worth doing, it is worth doing badly.

Literature is a luxury; fiction is a necessity.

Silence is the unbearable repartee.

There is nothing the matter with Americans except their ideals. The real American is all right; it is the ideal American who is all wrong.

Yawn: A silent shout.

Winston Churchill

A prisoner of war is a man who tries to kill you and fails, and then asks you not to kill him.

Democracy is the worst system devised by the wit of man, except for all the others.

He has all the virtues I dislike and none of the vices I admire.

He's a sheep in sheep's clothing.
— On political opponent Clement Attlee

In time of war, the truth is so precious it must be attended by a bodyguard of lies.

Communication

Mr. Speaker, if I had said that I would
not have been allowed to.
— British Member of Parliament

I waited
For the phone
To ring
And when at last
It didn't
I knew it was you.
— Eleanor Bron

I have nothing to say, and I'm saying it.
— John Cage

I have noticed that nothing I have never
said ever did me any harm.
— Calvin Coolidge

I will be so brief I have already finished.
— Salvador Dali, entire speech

Your very silence is your confession.
— Euripides

I guess I should warn you: If I turn out to be particularly clear, you've probably misunderstood what I said.
— Alan Greenspan

Don't forget to tell everyone: it's a secret.
— Gerald Lieberman

That's the most unheard of thing I ever heard of.
— Joseph McCarthy

It is impossible to speak in such a way that you cannot be misunderstood.
— Karl Popper

Don't think I'm not incoherent.
— Harold Ross, editor *New Yorker*

[T]here are known knowns; there are things we know that we know.
There are known unknowns; that is to say there are things that, we now know we don't know. But there are also unknown unknowns – there are things

we do not know, we don't know.
— Donald Rumsfeld

He has occasional flashes of silence that
make his conversation perfectly
delightful.
— Sydney Smith, on Lord Macaulay

The best way of answering a bad
argument is to let it go on.
— Sydney Smith

Well, if I called the wrong number, why
did you answer the phone?
— James Thurber, cartoon caption

I know you believe you understand what
you think I said, but I'm not sure you
realize that what you heard is not what
I meant.
— Unknown

I saw a store with this sign: "Specialists
in misleading advertising." When I went
in, I found they sold only plumbing

supplies.
— Unknown

Tact fails as soon as it's noticed.
— Unknown

We just don't discuss that capability. I can't tell you why we don't discuss it because then I'd be discussing it.
— Pete Williams, U.S. Defense Department spokesman

See also **Stanislaw Lec**

Death and Dying

It's not that I'm afraid to die. I just don't want to be there when it happens.
— Woody Allen

No one would go to Hitler's funeral if he was alive today.
— Ron Brown, British MP

If you don't go to other men's funerals,
they won't go to yours.
— Clarence Day

Once you're dead, you're made for life.
— Jimi Hendrix

It is too bad that dying is the last thing
we do, because it could teach us so much
about living.
— Robert Hershold

The meaning of life is that it stops.
— Franz Kafka

They say such nice things about people
at their funerals that it makes me sad to
realize that I'm going to miss mine by
just a few days.
— Garrison Keillor

Dying is a very dull, dreary affair. My
advice to you is to have nothing to do
with it.
— W. Somerset Maugham, supposedly
his last words

Die my dear doctor, that's the last thing
I shall do.
— Lord Palmerston

I wouldn't believe Hitler were dead,
even if he told me himself.
— Hjalmar Schacht, Hitler's central
bank governor, May 1945

The hour which gives us life begins to
take it away.
— Seneca

The dead carry with them to the grave
in their clutched hands only that which
they have given away.
— DeWitt Wallace

See also **Saki, Steven Wright**

Definitions

Celebrity: A person who is known for his
well-knownness.
— Daniel Boorstin

Fashion is made to become
unfashionable.
— Coco Chanelle

Circular Definition: See Definition,
Circular

To have no thoughts and be able to
express them – that's what makes a
journalist.
— Karl Kraus

Hope is the feeling we have that the
feeling we have is not permanent.
— Mignon McLaughlin

An economist: The only professional who
sees something working in practice and
then seriously wonders if it works in
theory.
— Ronald Reagan

Poverty: A sin that the rich cannot
forgive.
— Russian proverb

Boredom: The desire for desires.
— Leo Tolstoy

A bachelor: Someone who never makes
the same mistake twice.
— Unknown

Peter de Vries

Everybody hates me because I'm so
universally liked.

He could not forgive God for not
existing.

It is the final proof of God's omnipotence
that he need not exist in order to save
us.

The universe is like a safe to which
there is a combination. But the
combination is locked up in the safe.

The Domestic Scene

Cleaning anything involves making something else dirty, but anything can get dirty without making something else clean.
— Laurence Peter

An attic is where you store all the junk you'd throw away if you didn't have one.
— Herbert Prochnow

I washed a sock. Then I put it in the dryer. When I took it out, it was gone.
— Ron Schmidt

"Pieces of string too short to save" –
Label on a box of pieces of string, supposedly found in someone's attic (this story exists in numerous versions)
— Unknown

Education

The advantage of a classical education is

that it enables you to despise the wealth which it prevents you from achieving.
— Russell Green

A child's education should begin at least one hundred years before he is born.
— Oliver Wendell Holmes, Jr.

We are faced with the paradoxical fact that education has become one of the chief obstacles to intelligence and freedom of thought.
— Bertrand Russell

Math was my worst subject because I could never persuade the teacher that my answers were meant ironically.

— Calvin Trillin

They make you start school when you can't read or write and then tell you not to talk.
— Unknown

The English

An English lady on the Rhine hearing a German speaking of her party as foreigners, exclaimed: "No, we're not foreigners; we are English. It is you that are foreigners."
— Ralph Waldo Emerson

An Englishman, even if he is alone, forms an orderly queue of one.
— George Mikes

Boasting about modesty is typical of the English.
— George Bernard Shaw

The English have an extraordinary ability for flying into a great calm.
— Alexander Woollcott

Families

Parents are the last people on earth who

ought to have children.
— Samuel Butler

If your parents didn't have any children,
there's a good chance that you won't
have any.
— Clarence Day

Too many parents make life hard for
their children by trying, too zealously, to
make it easy for them.
— Goethe

The happiest parents are those without
children.
— Laurence Peter

The child is father of the man.
— William Wordsworth

Food

Never work before breakfast. If you
have to work before breakfast, get your

breakfast first.
— Josh Billings

What happens to the hole when the
cheese is gone?
— Bertolt Brecht

I'm not a *complete* vegetarian. I eat only
animals that have died in their sleep.
— George Carlin

"I'm so glad I don't like asparagus," said
the small girl to a sympathetic friend.
"Because if I did, I should have to eat it
– and I can't bear it!"
— Lewis Carroll

Yes, we have no bananas.
— Tad Dorgan, cartoon caption, later
used as a song title, by Irving Conn and
Frank Silver

One of the greatest unsolved riddles of
restaurant eating is that the customer
usually gets faster service when the

restaurant is crowded than when it is half empty; it seems that the less the staff has to do, the slower they do it.
— Sydney J. Harris

"My friend was like, 'Hey, you want a frozen banana?' 'No, but I want a regular banana later – so, yeah.'"
— Mitch Hedberg

The national dish of America is menus.
— Robert Robinson

Freedom

I need someone to protect me from all the measures they take in order to protect me.
— Banksy, street artist

If you think you're free, there's no escape possible.
— Baba Ram Dass

Liberty is always dangerous, but it is the safest thing we have.
— Henry Emerson Fosdick

My first act of free will shall be to believe in free will.
— William James

It's often safer to be in chains than to be free.
— Franz Kafka

It is true that liberty is precious – so precious that it must be rationed.
— Vladimir Ilyich Lenin

So Brother Matthew locked the gate behind me and I was enclosed in the four walls of my new freedom.
— Thomas Merton, on entering monastic life

We have to believe in free will. We've got no choice.
— Isaac Bashevis Singer

There is no need to struggle to be free;
the absence of struggle is in itself
freedom.
— Chögyam Trungpa

Liberty is the only thing you cannot
have unless you are willing to give it to
others.
— William Allen White

Samuel Goldwyn

A verbal contract isn't worth the paper
it's written on.

Any man who goes to a psychiatrist
should have his head examined.

I read part of it all the way through.

I don't think anybody should write his
autobiography until after he's dead.

I'm willing to admit that I may not always be right, but I am never wrong.

It rolls off my back like a duck.
— On criticism

Now why did you name your baby "John"? Every Tom, Dick and Harry is named "John."

The next time I send a damn fool for something, I go myself.

Health and Medicine

Can placebos cause side effects? If so, are the side effects real?
— George Carlin

Health nuts are going to feel stupid someday, lying in hospitals dying of nothing.
— Redd Foxx

It requires a great deal of faith for a man to be cured by his own placebos.
— John L. McClenahan

If you think health care is expensive now, wait until you see what it costs when it's free!
— P.J. O'Rourke

It should be the function of medicine to have people die young as late as possible.
— Ernst L. Wynder

History

Things have never been more like the way they are today in history.
— Dwight D. Eisenhower (also attributed to others)

The past is never dead. It's not even past.
— William Faulkner

The charm of history and its enigmatic lesson consist in the fact that, from age to age, nothing changes and yet everything is completely different.
— Aldous Huxley

"History repeats itself" and "History never repeats itself" are about equally true.
— G. M. Trevelyan

The farther backward you can look, the farther forward you are likely to see.
— Unknown

History is merely a list of surprises.... It can only prepare us to be surprised yet again.
— Kurt Vonnegut Jr.

I have always said it is a great mistake ever to pre-judge the past.
— William Whitelaw

See also **George Orwell, Saki**

Douglas Hofstadter

Hofstadter's Law: It always takes longer than you expect, even when you take Hofstadter's Law into account.

This sentence claims to be an Epimenides Paradox, but it is lying. *(See Epimenides quotation in "Logic, Truth and Lies")*

This sentence contradicts itself – or rather – well, no, actually it doesn't!

What should you do when told, "Disobey this command"?

Human Nature and Humankind

We are here on earth to do good for others. What the others are here for, I don't know.
— W. H. Auden

The defect of equality is that we only desire it with our superiors.
— Henry Becque

It is easier to forgive an enemy than to forgive a friend.
— William Blake

There are two kinds of people in this world: Those who divide everything into two groups, and those who don't.
— Kenneth Boulding

There are many who dare not kill themselves for fear of what the neighbors will say.
— Cyril Connolly

Some things that won't hurt you will scare you so bad that you hurt yourself.
— Boots Cooper

No people do so much harm as those who go about doing good.
— Bishop Mandell Creighton

We can never have enough of that which we do not want.
— Eric Hoffer

We have met the enemy and he is us.
— Walt Kelly's cartoon character, Pogo

To do just the opposite is also a form of imitation.
— Lichtenberg

It is an ironic habit of human beings to run faster when we have lost our way.
— Rollo May

Ask yourself whether you are happy and you cease to be so.
— John Stuart Mill

Until we lose ourselves, there is no hope of finding ourselves.
— Henry Miller

We are on the move from false certainty to true uncertainty.
— Henri Nouwen (attributed)

We are healed of a suffering only by
experiencing it to the full.
— Marcel Proust

If you try to please everybody,
somebody's not going to like it.
— Donald Rumsfeld

Anger's my meat; I sup upon myself,
And so shall starve with feeding.
— William Shakespeare, *Coriolanus*

We're all in this alone.
— Lily Tomlin

Identity

The reward for conformity was that
everyone liked you except yourself.
— Rita Mae Brown

She's a gay man trapped inside a
woman's body.
— Boy George, on Madonna

You've no idea what a poor opinion I have of myself, and how little I deserve it.
— W. S. Gilbert

Always remember that you are absolutely unique. Just like everyone else.
— Margaret Mead

A Chinaman of the T'ang dynasty – and by which definition, a philosopher – dreamed he was a butterfly, and from that moment he was never quite sure that he was not a butterfly dreaming it was a Chinese philosopher.
— Tom Stoppard (also attributed to others)

According to Senator Lott, if Ellen DeGeneres were a good Christian, she would have been born a heterosexual man.
— Unknown

Not many people realize just how well
known I am.
— Unknown

The Irish

When I came back to Dublin, I was
court-martialed in my absence and
sentenced to death in my absence, so I
said they could shoot me in my absence.
— Brendan Behan

When I told the people of Northern
Ireland I was an atheist, a woman in the
audience stood up and said, "Yes, but is
it the God of the Catholics or the God of
the Protestants in whom you don't
believe?"
— Quentin Crisp

You're not a proper member of an Irish
club until you've been barred.
— Michael Davitt

Half the lies they're telling about me aren't even true.
— Dublin politician

The only way to stop this suicide wave is to make it a capital offense, punishable by death.
— Irish legislator

Ah well, they say it's not as bad as they say it is.
— Irish woman on the Ulster situation

I ran after you, but when I caught up to you you'd gone.
— Irish saying

The Irish are a race of people who don't know what they want and are prepared to fight to the death to get it.
— Sidney Littlewood

Knowledge and Wisdom

Experts lie, say other experts
— Bizarro, cartoon headline

Son, I already know how to be twice as good a farmer as I am.
— A farmer, to a young agricultural extension agent

Only because
I err
Do I find
What I am not
Not looking for.
— Orides Fontela

The wisdom god, Woden, went out to the king of the trolls, got him in an armlock, and demanded to know of him how order might triumph over chaos. "Give me your left eye," said the troll, "and I'll tell you." Without hesitation Woden gave up his left eye. "Now tell me." The troll said, "The secret is 'Watch with both eyes.'"
— John Gardner

Ignorance is the key to everything in life. An ignorant person is constantly

surprised.
— Winston Groom, *Forrest Gump*

The little I know, I owe to my ignorance.
— Sacha Guitry

It is a self-flattering contradiction that wise men despise the opinions of fools, and yet are proud of having their esteem.
— Marquis of Halifax

My specialty is omniscience.
— Charles Haughey (attributed)

Wisdom is the quality that keeps you from getting into situations where you need it.
— Doug Larson

One day Soshi was walking on the bank of a river with a friend. "How delightfully the fishes are enjoying themselves in the water!" exclaimed Soshi. His friend spake to him thus: "You are not a fish; how do you know

that the fishes are enjoying themselves?" "You are not myself," returned Soshi; "how do you know that I do not know that the fishes are enjoying themselves?"
— Kakuzo Okakura

That theory is worthless. It isn't even wrong.
— Wolfgang Pauli, physicist

It is not wise to be wiser than necessary.
— Philippe Quinault

The only true wisdom is knowing you know nothing.
— Socrates

Duc de la Rochefoucauld

How can we expect another to keep our secret if we have been unable to keep it ourselves?

Plenty of people despise money but few know how to give it away.

The height of cleverness is being able to conceal it.

The love of justice in most men is simply the fear of suffering injustice.

We are all strong enough to bear the misfortunes of others.

Law, Lawyers and Justice

I have the kind of lawyer you hope the other fellow has.
— Raymond Chandler

We are in bondage to the law in order that we may be free.
— Cicero

At King's Lynn, Norfolk, yesterday, a man was granted legal aid when he

chose to go for trial on a charge of making a false statement for the purpose of obtaining free legal aid.
— English newspaper

The law, in its majestic equality, forbids the rich as well as the poor to sleep under bridges, to beg in the streets, and to steal bread.
— Anatole France

Capital punishment is our society's recognition of the sanctity of human life.
— Orrin Hatch

Who shall stand guard to the guards themselves? *(Sometimes translated as "Who will watch the watchmen?" or "Who will judge the judges?")*
— Juvenal

When two trains approach each other at a crossing, they shall both come to a full stop and neither shall start up until the other has gone.

— Kansas law, passed in the early 20th century

If a mime gets arrested is he informed of his right to remain silent?

— Jay Leno

The best way to get a bad law repealed is to enforce it strictly.

— Abraham Lincoln

A solicitor's account: To my professional charges for crossing the street to greet you, and on discovering that it was not you, crossing the street again: 25 guineas.

— Unknown English lawyer (probably apocryphal)

See also **Duc de La Rochefoucauld, Stanislaw Lec**

Laws of the Universe

Adding manpower to a late software project makes it later.
— Brooks' Law (from Fred Brooks, computer scientist)

There are no exceptions to the rule that everybody likes to be an exception to the rule.
— William F. Buckley

You're not late until you get there.
— Huhn's Law

Van Roy's Law: An unbreakable toy is useful for breaking other toys.
— Van Roy

Stanislaw Lec

Don't shout for help at night. You might wake your neighbors.

If a man who cannot count finds a four-leaf clover, is he lucky?

Sometimes you have to be silent to be heard.

The dispensing of injustice is always in the right hands.

The finger of God never leaves identical fingerprints.

Limericks

There was a young man from Japan
Whose limericks never would scan.
When asked why this was,
He said: "It's because
I always try and put as many words in the last line as I possibly can."

There once was a fellow named Wyatt
Whose voice was exceedingly quiet.
It faded away
Till eventually one day

....

There was a young lady of Crewe
Whose limericks stopped at line two.

There was a young man of Verdun.

Logic, Truth and Lies

Disregard this sign.

I am lying.
— One version of the "Liar paradox"

The statement written below is false.
The statement above is true.

This page intentionally left blank.

This sentence can never be proved.

The opposite of a correct statement is a
false statement. But the opposite of
profound truth may well be another
profound truth.
— Niels Bohr

I think sex is better than logic, but I can't prove it.
— Alan Dawson

All Cretans are liars.
— Epimenides of Crete

It is a double pleasure to deceive the deceiver.
— Jean de la Fontaine

Believe those who are seeking the truth. Doubt those who find it.
— André Gide

Things are not untrue just because they never happened.
— Dennis Hamley

I lie to myself all the time. But I never believe me.
— S. E. Hinton

One never trusts anyone that one has deceived.
— Jonathan Lynn and Antony Jay

Socrates in Troy says, "What Plato is now saying in Athens is false." At the same time, Plato in Athens says, "What Socrates is now saying in Troy is false."
— R. M. Sainsbury

If you want to be thought a liar, always tell the truth.
— Logan Pearsall Smith

Falsehood ceases to be falsehood when it is understood on all sides that the truth is not expected to be spoken.
— Henry Taylor

Anyone who says he's been eaten by a wolf is a liar.
— J. B. Theberge

See also **Winston Churchill**

Groucho Marx

I started out with nothing and I've still got most of it left.

Gentlemen: Please accept my resignation. I don't care to belong to any social organization that will accept me as a member.

If you fall out of that window and break both your legs, don't come running to me.

There is one way to find out if a man is honest: ask him. If he says "Yes," you know he is crooked.

Those are my principles and, if you don't like them . . . well, I've got others.

Who are you going to believe? Me, or your deceiving eyes?

Materialism and Money Matters

The only thing money gives is the freedom of not worrying about money.
— Johnny Carson

You cannot be insured for the accidents that are most likely to happen to you.
— Alan Coren

A bank is a place that will lend you money if you can prove that you don't need it.
— Bob Hope (also attributed to others)

The only wealth which you will keep forever is the wealth which you have given away.
— Martial

Sex is like money; only too much is enough.
— John Updike

I gave him an unlimited budget and he exceeded it.
— Edward Williams

Give me the luxuries of life and I will willingly do without the necessities.
— Frank Lloyd Wright

If what you are getting on-line is for free, you are not the customer, you are the product.
— Jonathan Zittrain

See also **Duc de La Rochefoucauld, Spike Milligan**

Memory and Memories

"It's a poor sort of memory that only works backwards," the Queen remarked.
— Lewis Carroll

I don't think I remember my first memory.
— Ellen DeGeneres

Should Auld Acquaintance be ... er ....
— Unknown

See also **Steven Wright**

Men and Women

A woman is a person who can look in a drawer and find a man's socks that aren't there.
— Dan Bennett

I'm so miserable without you
It's almost like having you here.
— Song title by Stephen Bishop

Married men make very poor husbands.
— Frank Crowninshield

I have always thought that every woman should marry, and no man.
— Benjamin Disraeli

The wife should be inferior to the husband. That is the only way to ensure equality between the two.
— Martial

When a man brings his wife a gift for no reason, there's a reason.
— Molly McGee

Spike Milligan

A man loses his dog, so he puts an ad in the paper. And the ad says, "Here, boy!"

A sure cure for seasickness is to sit under a tree.

All I ask is the chance to prove that money can't make me happy.

Silence when you speak to me!

Well, we can't stand around here doing nothing; people will think we're working.

Miscellaneous

You must understand that this is not a woman's dress I am wearing. It is a man's dress.
— David Bowie

In skating over thin ice, our safety is in
our speed.
— Ralph Waldo Emerson

I am currently boycotting so many
television shows that I may not have
time to boycott another.
— Nora Ephron

I think it's in my basement. Let me go
upstairs and check.
— M. C. Escher

One has two duties: to be worried and
not to be worried.
— E. M. Forster

[They] did nothing in particular
And did it very well.
— W. S. Gilbert

What about those red balls they have on
car aerials so you can spot your car in a
car park. I think all cars should have

them.
— Matt Groening's character, *Homer Simpson*

Those only deserve a monument who do not need one.
— William Hazlitt

There is no such thing as nothing.
— Martin Heidegger

I happen to admire the spirit of tolerance in our town. It's magnificent. Just don't forget that we have it because we all believe in the same thing.
— Henrik Ibsen, *An Enemy of the People*

My teacher says strangers are people we don't know. But that can't be true, because there are people who don't know us and we're not strangers.
— Robert Isaacs

The greatest thing since they reinvented sliced bread.
— William Keegan

R. A. Sorensen claims to have had a friend who objected to assigning chores by a random lottery, because that's biased in favor of lucky people.
— Robert M. Martin

Only a mediocre person is always at his best.
— W. Somerset Maugham

Practical people would be more practical if they would take a little more time for dreaming.
— J. P. McEvoy

As I was going up the stair
I met a man who wasn't there.
He wasn't there again today.
I wish, I wish, he'd stay away.
— Hughes Mearns

They laughed when I said I was going to be a comedian. They're not laughing now.
— Bob Monkhouse

Even when I was little, I was big.
— Football player William
"Refrigerator" Perry

He was cautious, but he was careful not
to show it.
— Frederic Raphael

In theory, there is no difference between
theory and practice; in practice, there is.
— Chuck Reid (also attributed to others)

If his father were alive today, he'd be
turning over in his grave.
— Leo Rosten

I'm an idealist. I don't know where I'm
going, but I'm on my way.
— Carl Sandburg

Members and non-members only
— Sign outside a Mexico City club

The butterfly flitting from flower to
flower ever remains mine, I lose the one

that is netted by me.
— Rabindranath Tagore

We who are liberal and progressive
know that the poor are our equals in
every sense except that of being equal to
us.
— Lionel Trilling

Look how strong I am; I can even show
that I'm weak.
— L. Weiss

A team effort is a lot of people doing
what I say.
— Michael Winner, British film director

Modern Society

Life is full of misery, loneliness,
unhappiness and suffering, and it's over
much too soon.
— Woody Allen

More than any time in history mankind faces a crossroads. One path leads to despair and utter hopelessness, the other to total extinction. Let us pray that we have the wisdom to choose correctly.
— Woody Allen

The trouble with our age is that it is all signpost and no destination.
— Louis Kronenberger

Two dangers constantly threaten the world: order and disorder.
— Paul Valéry

Murphy's Law

Anything that can go wrong, will go wrong.
— Murphy's Law (several variations exist)

Anything that can go wrong, will – at

the worst possible moment
— Finagle's Law

If Murphy's Law can go wrong, it will.
— Unknown

Murphy's Law only fails when you try to
demonstrate it.
— Unknown

Nature

Nature, to be commanded, must be
obeyed.
— Francis Bacon

A hen is only an egg's way of making
another egg.
— Samuel Butler

No cow's like a horse
And no horse like a cow.
That's one similarity, anyhow.
— Piet Hein

The universe may
Be as great as they say.
But it wouldn't be missed
If it didn't exist.
— Piet Hein

Dark is faster than light, otherwise
you'd see it.
— Unknown

Optimists and Pessimists

The optimist proclaims we live in the
best of all possible worlds, and the
pessimist fears this is true.
— James Branch Cabell

My pessimism goes the point of
suspecting the sincerity of the
pessimists.
— Jean Rostand

I'd like to be a pessimist but I'm afraid it
wouldn't work out.
— Unknown

But before rejecting pessimism, consider its pleasures. Pessimists are right more often than not, and when they are wrong they are pleased to be so.
— George Will

See also **Oscar Wilde**

George Orwell

All animals are equal but some animals are more equal than others.

All propaganda is lies, even when one is telling the truth.

The quickest way to end a war is to lose it.

There are some ideas so wrong that only a very intelligent person could believe in them.

Who controls the past controls the future.

Places

London is a splendid place to live for
those who can get out of it.
— Lord Balfour of Burleigh

In Israel, in order to be a realist you
must believe in miracles.
— David Ben Gurion

If you live in New York, even if you're
Catholic, you're Jewish.
— Lenny Bruce

Rome could neither bear its ills nor the
remedies that might have cured them.
— Livy

Much will have to change in Canada if
the country is to stay the same.
— Abraham Rotstein

Pink is the navy blue of India.
— Diana Vreeland

Power, Politics and Politicians

Politics is the gentle art of getting votes from the poor and campaign funds from the rich, by promising to protect each from the other.
— Oscar Ameringer

I don't know what he means, but I disagree with him.
— George H. W. Bush, responding to a journalist during the Gulf War

They misunderestimated me.
— George W. Bush

An honest politician is one who when he is bought will stay bought.
— Simon Cameron

We must restore to Chicago all the good things it never had.
— Mayor Richard Daley

Mr. Speaker, I withdraw my statement that half the cabinet are asses – half the cabinet are not asses.
— Benjamin Disraeli

Those who insist on the dignity of their office show they have not deserved it.
— Baltasar Gracián

Treason doth never prosper; what's the reason?
For if it prosper, none dare call it treason.
— John Harrington

It's ours. We stole it fair and square.
— Senator Samuel Hayakawa, on the Panama Canal Zone

It is essential to the triumph of reform that it should never succeed.
— William Hazlitt

Leaders are always failing somebody.
— Ronald A. Heifetz

The more power you give away, the more you have.
— Francis Hesselbein

When we got into office, the one thing that surprised me most was to find that things were just as bad as we'd been saying they were.
— John Kennedy

To lead, one must follow.
— Lao Tzu

Democracy gives every man the right to be his own oppressor.
— James Russell Lowell

Authority is like soap. The more you use it, the less you have.
— Luis Palau

I have made good judgments in the past. I have made good judgments in the future.
— Dan Quayle

However many you put to death, you will never kill your successor.
— Seneca, to the Emperor Nero

Mr. Churchill is easily satisfied with the best.
— F. E. Smith, on Winston Churchill

We are not without accomplishment. We have managed to distribute poverty equally.
— Nguyen Co Thach, Vietnamese foreign minister

Being powerful is like being a lady. If you have to tell people you are, you aren't.
— Margaret Thatcher

A year ago [President] Gerald Ford was unknown throughout America. Now he's unknown throughout the world.
— Unknown

A politician will always be there when

he needs you.
— Ian Walsh

He is going around the country stirring up apathy.
— William Whitelaw, on Harold Wilson

The Jews and Arabs should settle their dispute in the true spirit of Christian charity.
— Alexander Wiley

We enjoyed ... his slyness. He mastered the art of walking backward into the future. He would say, "After me." And some people went ahead, and some went behind, and he would go backward.
— Mikhail Zhvanetsky, on Mikhail Gorbachev

Problems and Problem Solving

There is no way to catch a snake that is as safe as not catching him.
— Jacob M. Braude

If there are obstacles, the shortest line between two points may be the crooked line.
— Bertolt Brecht

When you have exhausted all the possibilities, remember this – you haven't.
— Thomas Edison

The only way round is through.
— Robert Frost

The problem when solved will be simple.
— Charles Kettering

The solution to the problem changes the problem.
— John Peers

Our problems are mostly behind us – what we have to do now is fight the solutions.
— Alan P. Stults

Proverbs and National Sayings

Where there is no shame, there is no honor.
— Congolese proverb

Oh, the good old times when we were so unhappy.
— French saying

The more it changes, the more it remains the same.
— French saying

To endure what is unendurable is true endurance.
— Japanese proverb

Under capitalism man exploits man; under socialism the reverse is true.
— Polish proverb

How beautiful it is to do nothing, and then to rest afterwards.
— Spanish proverb

If the rich could hire other people to die for them, the poor could make a wonderful living.
— Yiddish proverb

See also **Definitions, Sleep, Time Warps**

Religion and Belief

He was of the faith chiefly in the sense that the church he currently did not attend was Catholic.
— Kingsley Amis

I understand it brings you luck whether you believe in it or not.
— Niels Bohr, asked if he believed the horseshoe above his door brought luck (several versions of this possibly apocryphal anecdote exist)

I don't believe in astrology. I'm a Sagittarian and we're skeptical.
— Arthur C. Clarke

The Christian church is a society of sinners. It is the only society in the world, membership in which is based upon the single qualification that the candidate shall be unworthy of membership.
— Charles Clayton Morrison

The Church of England is the perfect church for those who don't go to church.
— Gerald Priestland

Depend on the rabbit's foot if you will, but remember: it didn't work for the rabbit.
— R. E. Shay

By order of the King: "It is forbidden for God to work miracles here."
— Unknown, written at the entrance to a French cemetery that had been closed by King Louis XV because of some miracles that were supposedly resulting from the relics of someone buried there.

Can God make a rock too big for Him to lift?
— Unknown

Some people say there is a God. Others say there is no God. The truth probably lies somewhere in-between.
— W. B. Yeats

See also **Peter de Vries**

Saki (H. H. Munro)

Discipline to be effective must be optional.

The people of Crete make more history than they can consume locally.

The young man turned to him with a disarming candor, which instantly put him on his guard.

"Waldo is one of those people who would be enormously improved by death," said Clovis.

Sanity

Just because you're paranoid doesn't mean they aren't after you.
— Joseph Heller, *Catch 22*

There's a rule saying I have to ground anyone who's crazy.... There's a catch. Catch 22. Anyone who wants to get out of combat duty isn't really crazy.
— Joseph Heller, *Catch 22*

When dealing with the insane, it is best to pretend to be sane.
— Herman Hesse

Show me a sane man and I will cure him for you.
— Carl Jung

What sane person could live in this world and not be crazy?
— Ursula Le Guin

The doctors in a mental institution were thinking of releasing a certain schizophrenic patient. They decided to give him a lie detector test. One of the questions they asked him was, "Are you Napoleon?" He replied, "No." The machine showed he was lying.
— Raymond Smullyan

Sleep

The responsibility to nightmare is to wake up.
— Michael Harper

I fell asleep reading a dull book and I dreamed that I was reading on, so I awoke from sheer boredom.
— Heinrich Heine

Sleep faster, we need the pillows.
— Jewish saying

The amount of sleep required by the average person is five minutes more.
— Max Kauffman

You can't wake a person who is pretending to be asleep.
— Navajo proverb

The thought that it was time to go to sleep would waken me.
— Marcel Proust

See also **Yogi Berra**

Spatial Challenges

Don't try to stem the tide; move the beach.
— Wallace Bing

If you board the wrong train, it is no use running along the corridor in the other

direction.
— Dietrich Bonhoeffer

It takes all the running you can do just
to keep in the same place.
— Lewis Carroll

Come to think of it, you can't get there
from here.
— Marshall Dodge and Robert Bryan

We pierce doors and windows to make a
house; and it is on these spaces where
there is nothing that the usefulness of
the house depends. Therefore just as we
take advantage of what is, we should
recognize the usefulness of what is not.
— Lao Tzu

If you don't know where you are going,
you will end up somewhere else.
— Laurence Peter

I only point the way; a sign doesn't have
to go where it points.
— Max Scheler

No matter where you go, that's where
you'll be.
— Unknown

See also **Yogi Berra**

Sports, Games and Leisure

The action replay showed it to be worse
than it actually was.
— Ron Atkinson

Good fishing is just a matter of timing.
You have to get there yesterday.
— Milton Berle

An immortal said, "In playing chess,
there is no infallible way of winning, but
there is an infallible way of not losing."
He was asked what this infallible way
could be and replied, "It is not to play
chess."

— Feng Yulan

Golf is so popular simply because it is the best game in the world at which to be bad.
— A. A. Milne

Success and Failure

The toughest thing about success is that you've got to keep on being a success.
— Irving Berlin

There is an obvious cure for failure – and that is success. But what is the cure for success?
— Daniel Boorstin

He's completely unspoiled by failure.
— Noël Coward

The secret of success is sincerity. If you fake that you've got it made.
— Jean Giraudoux

He was a self-made man who owed his lack of success to nobody.
— Joseph Heller, *Catch 22*

My greatest fear for you is not that you will fail but that you will succeed in doing the wrong thing.
— Howard Hendricks

Each success only buys a ticket to a more difficult problem.
— Henry Kissinger

The way to succeed is to double your failure rate.
— Thomas Watson Jr.

Technology

Do you realize that if it weren't for Edison we'd be watching TV by candlelight?
— Al Boliska

Technological progress has merely provided us with a more efficient means of going backwards.
— Aldous Huxley

The greatest invention of the nineteenth

century was the invention of the method of invention.
— Alfred North Whitehead

The airplane stays up because it doesn't have the time to fall.
— Orville Wright

Thinking Things Through

We make our decisions, and then our decisions turn around and make us.
— F. W. Boreham

Sometimes I've believed as many as six impossible things before breakfast.
— Lewis Carroll, *Alice in Wonderland*

The supreme triumph of reason to is to cast doubt on its own validity.
— Miguel de Unamuno

All generalizations are dangerous, even this one.
— Alexander Dumas

All cases are unique and very similar to others.
— T. S. Eliot

When it is not necessary to make a decision, it is necessary not to make a decision.
— Lord Falkland

The test of a first-rate intelligence is the ability to hold two opposed ideas in mind at the same time and still retain the ability to function.
— F. Scott Fitzgerald

If you think you can do a thing or think you can't do a thing, you're right.
— Henry Ford

To be absolutely honest, what I feel really bad about is that I don't feel worse. There's the ineffectual liberal's problem in a nutshell.
— Michael Frayn

A liberal is a man too broad-minded to take his own side in a quarrel.
— Robert Frost

Few people have the imagination for reality.
— Goethe

And the trouble is, if you don't risk anything, you risk even more.
— Erica Jong

So many things are possible just as long as you don't know they're impossible.
— Norton Juster

Nothing is so useless as a general maxim.
— Thomas Macaulay

It is impossible to defeat an ignorant man in an argument.
— William Gibbs McAdoo

I have come to the conclusion, after many years of sometimes sad

experience, that you cannot come to any
conclusions at all.
— Vita Sackville-West

No one learns to make right decisions
without being free to make wrong ones.
— Kenneth Sollitt

Seek simplicity and then distrust it.
— Alfred North Whitehead

Time Warps

Time is a great teacher but
unfortunately it kills all its pupils.
— Hector Berlioz

To know the road ahead, ask those
coming back.
— Chinese proverb

Impatient people always arrive too late.
— Jean Dutourd

In times like these, it is helpful to
remember that there have always been
times like these.
— Paul Harvey

There's an art of knowing when.
Never try to guess.
Toast until it smokes and then
Twenty seconds less.
— Piet Hein

If you would civilize a man, begin with
his grandmother.
— Victor Hugo

You can only predict things after they've
happened.
— Eugene Ionesco

The trouble with being punctual is that
there's nobody there to appreciate it.
— Franklin P. Jones

Taste them again, for the first time.
— Slogan for Kellogg's Corn Flakes

Those who never have time do least.
— Lichtenberg

They announced on US TV that Patrick
MacNee, star of *The Avengers*, had died.
So they rang up my daughter in Palm
Springs. "Sorry to hear that your
father's dead." She said: "But I was
talking to him 12 minutes ago in
Australia." They said, "No he's dead –
it's just the time difference."
— Patrick MacNee

The future has to be lived before it can
be written about.
— Jawaharlal Nehru

The sooner you fall behind, the more
time you have to catch up.
— Sam Ogden

They spend their time mostly looking
forward to the past.
— John Osborne

Don't worry about the world coming to an end today. It's already tomorrow in Australia.
— Charles Schultz

A man with a watch knows what time it is. A man with two watches is never sure.
— Segal's Law

It's always easy the night before to get up early the next morning.
— Unknown

Never before has the future so rapidly become the past.
— Unknown

The trouble with our times is that the future is not what it used to be.
— Paul Valéry

See also **Steven Wright**

Travel

If you are sitting in an exit row and you cannot read this card or cannot see well enough to follow these instructions, please tell a crew member.
— Airplane safety pamphlet

We shall not cease from our explorations
And the end of all our exploring
Will be to arrive where we started
And know the place for the first time.
— T. S. Eliot

The average tourist wants to go to places where there are no tourists.
— Sam Ewing

A man travels the world over in search of what he needs and returns home to find it.
— George Moore

Sure, the next train has gone ten minutes ago.
— *Punch* magazine cartoon caption

To travel is to return to strangers.
— Dennis Scott

I dislike feeling at home when I'm
abroad.
— George Bernard Shaw

Sometimes one must travel far to
discover what is near.
— Uri Shulevitz

Wherever you travel, the weather is
"unusual for this time of year."
— Ruth J. Smock

Mark Twain (Samuel Clemens)

Giving up smoking is the easiest
thing in the world. I know because
I've done it thousands of times.

Education consists mostly in what we
have unlearned.

I have been told that Wagner's music is

better than it sounds.

The report of my death was an exaggeration.

The Great Unknown
(All sources unknown)

87 percent of statistics are made up on the spur of the moment.

All epigrams exaggerate – including this one.

Don't play stupid with me; I'm better at it.

Faculty flogging will continue until morale improves.

Fire exit – do not use.

Have you ever imagined a world with no hypothetical situations?

I went to buy some camouflage trousers but I couldn't find any.

I'd give my right arm to be ambidextrous.

If you leave me, can I come too?

Illiterate? Write for help to ….

Only the most foolish of mice would hide in a cat's ear. But only the wisest of cats would think to look there.

Please ensure that this gate is closed at all times.

She was like the old lady who once said she had suffered so much, especially from the troubles that never came.

The bigger the crowd, the more people show up for it.

The masochist: "Hurt me, hurt me."
The sadist: "No."

There are three kinds of people: those who are good with numbers and those who aren't.

What happens to your lap when you stand up?

Working here is like a nightmare. You'd like to get out of it but you need the sleep.

Values, Virtues and Vices

Men who are weak never give in when they should.
— Cardinal de Retz

Always try to do the right thing unless your conscience tells you otherwise.
— Winston Groom, *Forrest Gump*

Moderation is a virtue only in those who are thought to have no alternative.
— Henry Kissinger

You're not a nice guy if you have a gun, even if you are a nice guy.
— Edward Koch

We have reached the point where we cannot bear either our vices or their cure.
— Livy

Don't be humble. You're not that great.
— Golda Meir

I try to commit at least one deadly sin each day. If I don't get round to it, I can always chalk it up to sloth.
— Robert Ragno

The greatest cunning is to have none at all.
— Carl Sandburg

Whenever two good people argue over principles, they are both right.
— Marie von Ebner-Eschenbach

See also **Winston Churchill**

War and Peace

We make war that we can live in peace.
— Aristotle

One of the main reasons that it is so easy to march me off to war is that each of them feels sorry for the man next to him who will die.
— Ernest Becker

A conqueror is always a lover of peace.
— Karl von Clausewitz

We are going to have peace even if we have to fight for it.
— Dwight D. Eisenhower

We are doing everything we would normally be doing, but more of it.
— Israeli military spokesman on the army's state of alert

One more such victory and we are lost.
— Pyrrhus

It became necessary to destroy the village in order to save it.
— U.S. Army report on the razing of Ben Tre, South Vietnam, 1968

See also **Winston Churchill, George Orwell**

Oscar Wilde

Fashion is a form of ugliness so intolerable that we have to alter it every six months.

He hasn't an enemy in the world, and none of his friends like him.
— On George Bernard Shaw

Of course, if one had enough money to go to America, one wouldn't go.
— Said before a lucrative U.S. lecture tour

Pessimist: One, who, when he has the choice of two evils, chooses both.

There is only one thing in the world worse than being talked about, and that is not being talked about.

Wordplay

What's a question that contains the word "cantaloupe" for no apparent reason?
— John Allen Paulos

"Upon what subject?"
"The King."
"The King, sir, is not a subject."
— Daniel Purcell, renowned 17th century English punster on being asked to make a pun

A good pun is its own reword.
— Unknown

A man, a plan, a canal – Suez!
— Unknown, a "near miss" palindrome, based on "A man, a plan, a canal – Panama!"

How long is the answer to this question?
Ten letters.
— Unknown

I may be slow but I like non sequiturs.
— Unknown

This sentence would be seven words long
if it were six words shorter.
— Unknown

Steven Wright

I intend to live forever. So far, so good.

I took a course in speed-waiting. Now I
can wait an hour in only ten minutes.
Right now I'm having amnesia and déjà
vu at the same time. I think I've
forgotten this before.

Uh-oh, I've lost a buttonhole.

Writing

Sire, nothing is impossible for your majesty. Your majesty has set out to write bad verses and succeeded.
— Nicolas Boileau, noted poet and critic, when King Louis XIV sought his opinion on some verses he had written

Only the hand that erases can write the true thing.
— Meister Eckhart

If I had to give young writers advice, I'd say don't listen to writers talking about writing.
— Lillian Hellman

I know lots of $75-a-week writers, but they're all making $1,500 a week.
— Herman Mankiewicz

There are three rules for writing a novel. Unfortunately, no one knows what they are.
— W. Somerset Maugham

You say there is nothing to write about.
Then write to me that there is nothing
to write about.
— Pliny the Younger

God lets you write; he also lets you not
write.
— Kurt Vonnegut Jr.

Zen sayings

Scratch first, itch later.

To make a vase, you need both clay and
the absence of clay.

When you reach the top, keep climbing.

Zen is like looking for the spectacles that
are sitting on your nose.

INDEX

Dublin politician — **The Irish**
Dumas, Alexander — **Thinking Things Through**
Dutourd, Jean — **Time Warps**

Eckhart, Meister — **Writing**
Edison, Thomas — **Problems and Problem Solving**
Eisenhower, Dwight D. — **History; War and Peace**
Eliot, T. S. — **Thinking Things Through; Travel**
Emerson, Ralph Waldo — **The English; Miscellaneous**
English newspaper — **Law, Lawyers and Justice**
Ephron, Nora — **Miscellaneous**
Epimenides of Crete — **Logic, Truth and Lies**
Escher, M. C. — **Miscellaneous**
Euripides — **Communication**
Ewing, Sam — **Travel**

Falkland, Lord — **Thinking Things Through**
Farrell, James T. — **America and Americans**
Faulkner, William — **History**
Feng Yulan — **Sports, Games and Leisure**
Finagle — **Murphy's Law**
Fitzgerald, F. Scott — **Thinking Things Through**
Fontela, Orides — **Knowledge and Wisdom**
Ford, Henry — **Thinking Things Through**
Forster, E. M. — **Miscellaneous**
Fosdick, Henry Emerson — **Freedom**
Foxx, Redd — **Health and Medicine**
France, Anatole — **Law, Lawyers and Justice**
Frayn Michael — **Thinking Things Through**
French saying — **Proverbs and National Sayings**
Friedenberg, Edgar Z. — **America and Americans**
Frost Robert — **Problems and Problem Solving;
    Thinking Things Through**

Gardner, John — **Knowledge and Wisdom**
George, Boy — **Identity**
Gide, André — **Logic, Truth and Lies**

Gilbert, W. S. — **Identity; Miscellaneous**
Gillespie, Dizzy — **The Arts**
Giraudoux, Jean — **Success and Failure**
Goethe — **Families; Thinking Things Through**
Goldwyn, Samuel — **See section under this heading**
Gracián, Baltasar — **Power, Politics and Politicians**
Green, Russell — **Education**
Greenspan, Alan — **Communication**
Groening, Matt — **Miscellaneous**
Groom, Winston — **Knowledge and Wisdom; Values, Virtues and Vices**
Guitry, Sacha — **Knowledge and Wisdom**

Hadas, Moses — **Books and Reading**
Halifax, Marquis of — **Knowledge and Wisdom**
Hamley, Dennis — **Logic, Truth and Lies**
Harper, Michael — **Sleep**
Harrington, John — **Power, Politics and Politicians**
Harris Sydney J. — **Food**
Harvey, Paul — **Time Warps**
Hatch, Orrin — **Law, Lawyers and Justice**
Haughey, Charles — **Knowledge and Wisdom**
Hayakawa, Samuel — **Power, Politics and Politicians**
Hazlitt, William — **Miscellaneous; Power, Politics and Politicians**
Hedberg, Mitch — **Food**
Heidegger, Martin — **Miscellaneous**
Heifetz, Ronald A. — **Power, Politics and Politicians**
Hein, Piet — **Nature; Time Warps**
Heine, Heinrich — **Sleep**
Heller, Joseph — **Sanity; Success and Failure**
Hellman, Lillian — **Writing**
Hendricks, Howard — **Success and Failure**
Hendrix, Jimi — **Death and Dying**
Heraclitus — **Change**
Hershold, Robert — **Death and Dying**

MacNee, Patrick — **Time Warps**
Mankiewicz, Herman — **Writing**
Martial — **The Arts; Materialism and Money Matters; Men and Women**
Martin, M. Robert — **Appearances; Books and Reading; Miscellaneous**
Marx, Groucho — **See section under this heading**
Maugham, W. Somerset — **Death and Dying; Miscellaneous; Writing**
May, Rollo — **Human Nature and Humankind**
McAdoo, William Gibbs — **Thinking Things Through**
McCarthy, Joseph — **Communication**
McClenahan, John L. — **Health and Medicine**
McEvoy, J. P. — **Miscellaneous**
McGee, Molly — **Men and Women**
McGinley Phyllis — **The Arts**
McLaughlin, Mignon — **Definitions**
Mead, Margaret — **Identity**
Mearns, Hughes — **Miscellaneous**
Meir, Golda — **Values, Virtues and Vices**
Merton, Thomas — **Freedom**
Mikes, George — **The English**
Mill, John Stuart — **Human Nature and Humankind**
Miller, Henry — **Human Nature and Humankind**
Miller, Irwin — **Ages and Aging**
Milligan, Spike — **See section under this heading**
Milne, A. A. — **Sports, Games and Leisure**
Monkhouse, Bob — **Miscellaneous**
Moore, George — **Travel**
Morrison, Charles Clayton — **Religion and Belief**

Nash, Ogden — **Change**
Navajo proverb — **Sleep**
Nehru, Jawaharlal — **Time Warps**
Nouwen, Henri — **Human Nature and Humankind**

O'Rourke, P.J. — **Health and Medicine**

Ogden, Sam — **Time Warps**
Okakura, Kakuzo — **Knowledge and Wisdom**
Orwell, George — **See section under this heading**
Osborne, John — **Time Warps**

Palau, Luis — **Power, Politics and Politicians**
Palmerston, Lord — **Death and Dying**
Pauli, Wolfgang — **Knowledge and Wisdom**
Paulos, John Allen — **Wordplay**
Peers, John — **Problems and Problem Solving**
Perry, William — **Miscellaneous**
Peter, Laurence — **The Domestic Scene**; **Families;**
  Spatial Challenges
Phillpotts, Eden — **Advice**
Picasso, Pablo — **The Arts**
Pliny the Younger — **Writing**
Polish proverb — **Proverbs and National Sayings**
Popper, Karl — **Communication**
Priestland, Gerald — **Religion and Belief**
Prochnow, Herbert — **The Domestic Scene**
Proust, Marcel — **Human Nature and Humankind;**
  Sleep
Punch magazine — **Travel**
Purcell, Daniel — **Wordplay**
Pyrrhus — **War and Peace**

Quayle, Dan — **Power, Politics and Politicians**
Quinault, Philippe — **Knowledge and Wisdom**

Ragno, Robert — **Values, Virtues and Vices**
Raphael, Frederic — **Miscellaneous**
Reagan, Ronald — **Definitions**
Reid, Chuck — **Miscellaneous**
Robinson, Robert — **Food**
Rogers, Carl — **Change**
Ross, Harold — **Communication**
Rostand, Jean — **Optimists and Pessimists**

Rosten, Leo — **Miscellaneous**
Rotstein, Abraham — **Places**
Rumsfeld, Donald — **Communication**; **Human Nature and Humankind**
Russell, Bertrand — **Education**
Russell, Lord John — **Appearances**
Russian proverb — **Definitions**

Sackville-West, Vita — **Thinking Things Through**
Sainsbury, R. M. — **Logic, Truth and Lies**
Saki (H. H. Munro) — **See section under this heading**
Sandburg, Carl — **Miscellaneous**; **Values, Virtues and Vices**
Saudi Arabian government — **Change**
Schacht, Hjalmar — **Death and Dying**
Scheler, Max — **Spatial Challenges**
Schmidt, Ron — **The Domestic Scene**
Schnabel, Arthur — **The Arts**
Schultz Charles — **Time Warps**
Scott, Dennis — **Travel**
Segal — **Time Warps**
Seneca — **Death and Dying**; **Power, Politics and Politicians**
Shakespeare, William — **Human Nature and Humankind**
Shaw, George Bernard — **The English**; **Travel**
Shay, R. E. — **Religion and Belief**
Shulevitz, Uri — **Travel**
Silver, Frank — **Food**
Singer, Isaac Bashevis — **Freedom**
Smith, F. E. — **Power, Politics and Politicians**
Smith, Logan Pearsall — **Logic, Truth and Lies**
Smith, Sydney — **Books and Reading**; **Communication**
Smock, Ruth J. — **Travel**
Smullyan, Raymond — **Books and Reading**; **Sanity**
Socrates — **Knowledge and Wisdom**

Sollitt, Kenneth — **Thinking Things Through**
Spanish proverb — **Proverbs and National Sayings**
Stein, Gertrude — **America and Americans**
Stoppard, Tom — **Ages and Aging**; **Identity**
Stults, Alan P. — **Problems and Problem Solving**
Sullivan, Frank — **Appearances**

Tagore, Rabindranath — **Miscellaneous**
Taylor, Henry — **Logic, Truth and Lies**
Thach, Nguyen Co — **Power, Politics and Politicians**
Thatcher, Margaret — **Power, Politics and Politicians**
Theberge, J. B. — **Logic, Truth and Lies**
Thurber, James — **Communication**
Tolstoy, Leo — **Definitions**
Tomlin, Lily — **Human Nature and Humankind**
Trevelyan, G. M. — **History**
Trillin, Calvin — **Education**
Trilling, Lionel — **Miscellaneous**
Trungpa, Chögyam — **Freedom**
Twain, Mark (Samuel Clemens) — **See section under this heading**

U.S. Army report — **War and Peace**
Updike, John — **Materialism and Money Matters**
Ustinov, Peter — **The Arts**

Valéry, Paul — **Modern Society**; **Time Warps**
Van Roy — **Laws of the Universe**
von Ebner-Eschenbach, Marie — **Values, Virtues and Vices**
Vonnegut, Kurt Jr. — **History**; **Writing**
Vreeland, Diana — **Places**

Wallace, DeWitt — **Death and Dying**
Walsh, Ian — **Power, Politics and Politicians**
Watson, Thomas Jr. — **Success and Failure**

Weiss, L. — **Miscellaneous**

Welles, Orson — **The Arts**

White, Phil — **Appearances**

White, William Allen — **Freedom**

Whitehead, Alfred North — **Technology; Thinking Things Through**

Whitelaw, William — **History; Power, Politics and Politicians**

Wilde, Oscar — **See section under this heading**

Wiley, Alexander — **Power, Politics and Politicians**

Will, George — **Optimists and Pessimists**

Williams, Edward — **Materialism and Money Matters**

Williams, Pete — **Communication**

Winner, Michael — **Miscellaneous**

Woollcott, Alexander — **The English**

Wordsworth, William — **Families**

Wright, Frank Lloyd — **Materialism and Money Matters**

Wright, Orville — **Technology**

Wright, Steven — **See section under this heading**

Wynder, Ernst L. — **Health and Medicine**

Yeats, W. B. — **Religion and Belief**

Yiddish proverb — **Proverbs and National Sayings**

Zhvanetsky, Mikhail — **Power, Politics and Politicians**

Zittrain, Jonathan — **Materialism and Money Matters**

About The Compiler

Sleep Faster, We Need The Pillows is Gordon Jackson's sixth anthology of quotations. Orginally from South Africa, he has taught journalism and worked in academic adminstration at Whitworth University, in Spokane, WA, since 1983.

He completed his undergraduate work at the University of Cape Town. He also has an MA from Wheaton College and a doctorate in mass communication from Indiana University. He worked as a journalist in Johannesburg in the 1970s.

Jackson is married to another South African, Sue, who he says helps keep his accent honest. They have two adult children, Sarah and Matthew.

15058697R00074

Made in the USA
Charleston, SC
15 October 2012